THE CASE OF OUR AFFAIRES

IN LAW, RELIGION, AND OTHER CIRCUMSTANCES

by

JOHN SPELMAN

Published by *The Rota* at the University of Exeter
1975

© *The Rota*, 1975
ISBN 0 904617 03 3

Printed in Great Britain by
The Printing Unit of the University of Exeter

Bibliographical Note

The case of our affaires is one of the royalist replies to Henry Parker's *Observations upon some of his majesties late answers and expresses* London, 1642, reprinted by W. Haller in *Tracts on liberty* (New York, 1933), II, 165-213. The controversy had originated with the king's *Answer to the nineteen propositions* in June 1642. That manifesto emanated from the king's moderate civilian advisers;Clarendon tells us that it was composed by Falkland and Colepeper. The *Answer* characterised the parliamentary demands as subversive to the 'ancient, equal, happy, well-poised and never-enough commended Constitution of this Kingdom', in which monarchy, aristocracy and democracy were mixed so as to secure the benefits and avoid the ills of the pure forms. Furthermore the *Answer* while emphasising the king's executive and military powers and refusing 'to make our Self, of a King of England, a Duke of Venice, and this of a Kingdom, a Republick', admitted that the laws were 'jointly made by a King, by a House of Peers, and by a House of Commons chosen by the People, all having free Votes and particular Priviledges'. Parker's *Observations* went beyond this admission of an independent constitutional position for the houses of parliament in asserting that the king's fiduciary powers in government were derived from the people and were to be used for the benefit of the people. Moreover, the power of the people was embodied in parliament.

Sir John Spelman countered Parker's doctrine of popular sovereignty exercised by the houses of parliament by reasserting the sovereignty of the king—'there neither is, nor can be any co-ordination, nor co-equalitie of any Estate, Order, or Degree, of the Subject with the Soveraigne' (below, pp. 2-3). Yet Spelman admitted that the king was not absolute but constitutionally restrained to act in certain regular ways; for example, he can only make law with the consent of the nobles and the commons. Spelman's vindication of this view of the English constitution relies on legal and historical evidence. He apparently inherited a love of history from his father, Sir Henry Spelman, the antiquary. For an account of this constitutional controversy, see C. C. Weston, *English constitutional theory and the house of lords, 1556-1832* (New York and London, 1965), pp. 23-43; on royalist thought 1642-44, there is a brief discussion by J. W. Allen, *English Political Thought, 1603-1660* (London, 1938), I, 482-519.

Summoned by the king to Oxford, Spelman not only engaged in political pamphleteering but also attended the royal council. He died of camp fever in July 1643 before he could be appointed one of the secretaries of state and before publication of *The case of our affaires*.

Three versions of the pamphlet exist. See F. Madan, *Oxford Books* (Oxford, 1912), II, 310-311. The earliest, (Madan 1516) was printed in Oxford, probably by Henry Hall. It includes 'A discoverie of Londons obstinacie and miserie' on pp. 32-38; and its p. 11 begins, 'therefore the most'. This is the version here reprinted. Presumably it was published before the variant collected by Thomason on 29 January 1643/44 (Madan 1517) which was printed in London although it purports to come from Oxford. Less generously produced (26 pp.), it prudently omitted the distribe against London; its p. 11 begins 'which we could'. The third variant (Madan 1518) has a title page and printer's ornaments identical to the second, but it has been reset with a number of printing changes; its final word is 'condition' instead of 'destruction'.

The case of our affaires is reproduced by permission of the Curators from a copy in the Bodleian Library, shelf mark C. 14. 4. Linc; Wing S4935.

The Case of our Affaires,
IN
LAW,
RELIGION,

And other Circumstances briefly Examined, and Presented to the
CONSCIENCE.

Auth: D^no Joh:
Spelmā Hen.
filio.

Printed in the Yeare, 1643.

(1)

The Case of our Affaires in Law, Religion, and other Circumstances briefly examined, &c.

Hough the Bonds of all Dutie are originally and principally founded in God, and tied by Religion; yet seeing all civill Duties relate to the particularitie of the humane Ordinance, and according to the nature of it, is with more or lesse importance to be exacted. What Subject soever would finde the true rule and bond of his obedience, must in the first place look what the State is wherein he lives, and in whom the Soveraignitie is to which his obedience and faith is inevitably bound.

Our State of *England* (even by the declaration of our Lawes) is a Kingdom, an Empire, a well regulated Monarchie; the Head thereof a Supreme Head, a Soveraigne, a King whose Crown is an Imperiall Crown, the Kingdom *His* Kingdom, *His* Realme, *His* Dominion, the People *His* People, the Subject *His* Subject, not onely as they are single men, but even when being in Parliament assembled; they make the Bodie Representative of the whole Kingdom considered apart without the King, so that the very Parliament it selfe is also by our Lawes called *His* Parliament : the King alone by Law hath power to call together in Parliament that Representative Bodie, and at His pleasure to dissolve it; He personally hath Homage and Oath of fidelitie of all the Peeres as of *His* Barons, and all the Commons in Parliament do by Law swear Alleageance to Him as to the *Onely Supreme Governour, and to assist and defend all Jurisdictions, Privi ledges, Preheminences, and Authorities, belonging to Him, His Heires and Successours, or annexed to the Imperiall Crown of the Realme.*

25. H. 8.
cap. 22.
24 H 8.
cap. 12.
26. H. 8.
cap. 2.
1. Eliz. 1.
1. Iac. 1.
Co. 5.
Cawdry case,
fol. 9. b.
vide the
Parl. writ.

1 Eliz. 1.
& 5 Eliz.

A 2   By

By the same Oath also is every Officer of considerable trust in Church and Common-wealth assured to His Majestie; and not onely they, but every single man of twelve yeares of age ought by Law in some or other of His Majesties Leetes to swear Alleageance to His Majestie: and never in our Law have we known an Oath of obedience to be made unto the Parliament, or any other Power in any case, either of mis-government or danger, how extraordinary soever.

This Soveraignitie in the King appeares not onely by that Oath of Supremacie, but by the constant acknowledgement of our Acts of Parliament both antient and moderne, which alwayes stile the King *Our Soveraigne Lord the King*, that is, not Soveraigne Lord to every single man onely (as the Observer traiterously and foolishly would make it) but the universalitie of us, even to our Bodie Representative in Parliament. For we must note that though we have among us many that are called Lords even by our Acts of Parliament themselves, yet being Lords without relation to the communitie or publique they are never called *Our Lords*, but *The Lords*, with addition of such or such place or Office; and they indeed are Lords *singulis*, not *universis*, for every particular man may call such a Lord *My Lord*, but the Communitie may not call him *Our Lord*, for to be Our Lord is to be Lord of the Communitie, and that belongeth onely to *Our Soveraigne Lord the King*.

Our very Acts of Parliament declaring this State to be a right Imperiall Kingdom, a Kingdom (we know) consisteth of no more than two formall parts onely, that is to say, a Soveraigne Head, and a Subject Bodie; and then it clearly followeth that what cooperation soever there be of any of the Members with the Head for the doing of any necessary Act of State, whatsoever necessitie there be of the concurrence of those Members; and howsoever they may seem to be Parties, Orders, or States, co-equally authorised in the power of acting with the Head, yet plainly there neither is, nor can be any co-ordination, nor co-equalitie of any Estate, Order, or Degree, of the Subject

with

with the Soveraigne, nor any competition of the Subjects power (in his concurrence) with the virtuall and primary influence of the Soveraignes power; but a plain subordination and subjected ministration of the one under the Soveraignitie of the other, as in the further examination of their differing interests will manifestly appear.

We see the Soveraignitie of this State clearly vested in the King, by Law established in Him, and inseparably annexed to His Person, by which He hath also inseparably both the Soveraigne power and Soveraigne judgement: but as in judging and determining matters of private interest, His power is not absolute, but is restrained to judgement, (not judgement arbitrary in His own Person but judgement to be administred by the proper sworne Judges of His Courts of Law) so in matters of publique affaire, for so much as concernes the making of Law; His power and judgement are so restrained to the concurrence of the Nobles, and Commons in Parliament, as that He cannot make any settled Law without their consent: but then in all other things that are not expresly restrained by any Law, as in providing for the present safetie against suddain danger, which Senates are so unapt to do, as that the famous *Roman* Senate was ever fain to choose a *Dictator* to do it for them; likewise in levying of Armes, suppressing of tumults and rebellions, convoaking of Parliaments, and dissolving of them, making of Peeres, granting libertie of sending Burgesses to Parliament, treating with Forraigne States, making of War, League, and Peace, granting safe conduct and protection, indenizing, giving of Honour, rewarding, pardoning, coyning, and the like: in all these and divers other points of Regalitie, the Soveraignitie both of judgement and power ever hath been and still is in the King alone, freely and at his own discretion is secured to him by the Oath of Supremacie, whereby as aforesaid, the vvhole Representative of Commons, all Magistrates and men in place both in Church and Common-vvealth svvear *To assist and defend all jurisdictions, priviledges, prebeminences, and authorities belonging*

Lo. Chal Egertons Post nati 73.b:

Psal.60,7.
Gen.49.10
Deut.33.
4. & 5.

longing to the Kings. For it is plain, that seeing that by the Lavv of God and Nations, to be King is to be Supreme Judge and Lavv-giver; vvhosoever is King is supreme in every thing vvherein he is not especially restrained, and his restraint being by the peculiar Lavves of his Kingdome, he can be no further restrained than the knovvn Lavves thereof expresly manifest.

The great restraint of regall absolutenesse in our State is in the tvvo points of declaring and making of Lavv, in neither of vvhich doth the King depart vvith any vvhit of his Soveraignitie. In the point declaring of Lavv, the King is restrained ordinarily to the mediation of his Judges, vvho to declare the Lavv by deliverie of the genuine sense and interpretation of Lavv according to to art and rules of science, are in their respective Courts the proper and authorised Judges, and Interpreters of Law, and do by their interpretation and judgement then binde both the King and Subject.

Lo. Cha.
Egertons
Post nati
fol 22. &
23 sect.4

Next above them upon errour supposed in their judgement, the House of Lords (who anciently were exercised in the Lawes and learned in them, and are assisted with all or most of the Judges of the Benches) do upon Writs of Errour in Parliament revise, and by the advice of the Judges affirme or reverse the Sentence of the next inferiour Courts, where the judgement whither given for the King or for a common person, may be reversed, and as well the King as the common person bound by their reversall and judgement, unlesse they be relieved by expresse Act of Parliament.

Other way of Declaring Law, in true proprietie of speech (that is, to declare the genuine sense and dictate of the Law as it naturally ariseth from the force of Lawes in being) there is none: for as for declaring Law by Act of Parliament, though that of all other be most authentique, yet it is not authentique for acurate judgement in interpretation supposed to be in the two Houses there, so much as for authoritie legislative administred by the three Orders of that high Court: for should the three Orders declare Law contrary to what were Law indeed,

yet

yet could not their Declaration be erroneous, for that it thenceforth altered the Law and made their dictate Law though it were none before. Such Declaration of Law therefore being never possible to be made but by the full legislative power of all the three Orders, is not so properly a Declaring or interpreting of Law, as rather the making of it, and is therefore to be referred to the point of restraint in making of Law. And this is clear that in such declaring of Law the Kings power is so much lesse restrained than it is by declaring of Law by their inferiour Courts as that in this he himselfe hath ever a personall Vote in the Declaration, but in other he hath none at all.

As to the restraint of regall absolutenesse in point of making Law. When our wise and pious Christian Princes had once brought the Kingdom to an happy frame of just and regular Government, and sought by all meanes the establishment of that good condition, which promised both prosperitie to their people, and stabilitie to their own Dominion. (Change and Innovation being thenceforth more to be feared than any other thing) They for preservation of what they had done, began to yeild the absolutenesse of their power, without which they could never have brought the State into any perfect frame, unto some retardation of motion, and regulation of power; and came by degrees not onely to use the advice of the Bishops and Barons in making of their Lawes, but their consents also; and then not onely their advice and consents, but the advice and consents of the Commons also; condescending at last that as to the power of making Law, their Scepter should thenceforth be locked up under the cautelous ward of a triple hand; so as no new Act whatsoever should obtain the Authoritie of a positive Law without the agreement of the King, the Peeres, and the Commons; to the end that no unadvised Law, not well examined and found agreeing with the interests of every of the three formall parts of this Kingdom, might in any part maime or enfeeble the established frame; which yet did not so much coop up or curbe the regall power from any due worke or office

office that belongeth to it; as rather clofe and fence it in, within the bounds of safetie and of prefervation.

Now this reftraint being at firft collaterall and accidentall to the Soveraigne power, did not in the beginning otherwife binde our Princes than by their voluntary and pious fubmiffion of their wils, till conftant cuftome becomming a Law made that ufage which was at firft at their will, become an abfolute and inevitable limitation of their power, fo as that at this day no pofitive Law can now be made by the King, without the confent of the Peeres and of the Commons: and yet for all this neceffitie now of their concurrence and confent, nor any part of the Soveraignitie (to which the legiflative power is infeperably incident) is in any fort transferred, or communicate unto them: but as in our Copy hold Eftates, the Copy holder of a meer Tenant at Will, comes by cuftome to gain a cuftomary inheritance, and fo to limit and reftrain the will and power of the Lord, as that he cannot make any determination of the Copyholders eftate otherwife than according to the cuftome of the Mannour: yet does not he deprive the Lord of his Lordfhip in the Copy hold, nor participate with him in it, neither yet deveft the Fee and Frank-tenement out of the lord, but they ftill remain in him and are ever parcell of the Lords Demeafne. So in this reftraining of the Kings legiflative power to the concurrence of the Peeres and Commons: though the cuftome of the Kingdom hath fo fixed and fettled the reftraint, as that now the King cannot in that point ufe his foveraigne power without the concurrence of the Peeres and Commons according to the cuftome of the Kingdom, yet ftill the Soveraignitie (and with it the infeperable legiflative power) does foly refide in the King. As for the Peeres and Commons they being meerly Inftruments of Regulation and qualification of the Kings legiflative abfolutenefle, are no fharers with him in the Soveraignitie, but alwayes remain (as our very legiflative Acts of Parliament do alwayes fpeak them) *His Majefties Subjects*. And His Majeftie for all this reftraining power of theirs remaines (as they themfelves themselves in the legiflative Acts, and not without an Oath, acknowledge Him their *true and onely Soveraigne*.

Apparantly therefore the Soveraignitie or regall power being thus in matters of private intereft reftrained to the rule, jurifdiction, and adminiftration of Law, as well by inferiour Courts as by the Houfe of Lords; and in the publique affaire of making Law, reftrained to the concurrence of the Peers and Commons, is not fo properly faid to be reftrained, as regulated. For neither is any of the Kings juft and neceffary power to the prejudice of the Crown taken from Him (for the Law in no fort fuffers any diminution of the juft and due Soveraignitie) neither is there any partenerfhip of the Supremacie thereby thruft upon the King, when the Law, notwithftanding the reftraint exprefly declares Him *The onely Supreme Governour*. Neither yet is any of the irregular and exorbitant abfolutenefle, which the Law feparates from the regalitie, any way transferred to the Courts or perfons that are the inftrumentals of the regulation, but the Law feparating all irregular licentioufneffe from the Regalitie, utterly annihilates and makes null all practice and exercife thereof. In fumme, all that is effected by this regulation is, the King as He ever was, fo ftill remaines, wholly and foly Soveraigne of the Kingdom onely, not of a licentious and illegall, but of a regular and legitimate Dominion.

But when the power and authoritie of Parliament is acknowledged to be the higheft, moft abfolute, and moft Soveraigne power in the Kingdom, and feemes repugnant to that which we have alleadged, that the Soveraignitie is wholly and foly in the King; We fhall eafily reconcile that apparition of contradiction, if we confider that we ufe the word Parliament to divers fenfes, and that in two fenfes wherein we ufe the word Parliament there is no Soveraignitie to be afcribed to it.

We fometimes ufe the word Parliament for the Houfe of Lords onely. As when upon Writs of Errour any Judgement in the Kings Bench is examined in the Houfe of Lords, and there affirmed or reverfed, the Judgement is faid to be affirmed or reverſed by Parliament. And yet though in that ſenſe, the Houſe of Lords is well enough called The Parliament, yet is it not the high Court of Parliament, which is the ſupreme Judgement, power, and Authoritie of the Kingdome, and that we may eaſily ſee in this, that though the Lords have power there to reverſe the Judgements of their inferiour Courts, yet have they not power to reverſe their own Judgements, nor to reſtore again any Judgement that they have reverſed; for they judging miniſterially, and not ſoveraignely, do as well binde their own hands as the hands of their inferiours, whereas the abſolute ſoveraigne power doth not ſo, but may reverſe any judgement that they themſelves have given, and again reſtore the judgement that they themſelves reverſed, for the abſolute ſupreme Court having *Juris dandi dictionem*, can never be at the laſt period of her juriſdiction; but looking ever forward to the preſent occaſion, whatſoever paſſed before, it *pro re nata* legiſlatively judgeth, maketh, and declareth Law. But the Houſe of Lords (though the moſt ſuperiour of all Courts of miniſteriall iuriſdiction) and all other inferiour Courts, (they having no other iuriſdiction than onely *juris dati dictionem*,) in uſing their iuriſdiction do conſummate it, and bring it to a period, beyond which they cannot go. Beſides the Houſe of Lords is not univerſally to all occaſions a iudicatorie, and therefore not ſoveraigne, but is the diſtinct Court of the Kings Barons of Parliament of particular and miniſteriall iuriſdiction, in which the King (though one of the three Voters in Parliament) yet in thoſe things which come by proceſſe of Law to receive determination there onely, hath no Vote at all, no more than in all other Courts of miniſteriall iuriſdiction.

Sometime we uſe the word Parliament for the two Houſes of Parliament onely, and that in regard they are the groſſe of the Bodie, whereof the Parliament conſiſts, there wanting onely the Soveraigne Head to compleat it. But the two Houſes alone without the King are ſo farre from being the ſupreme and high Court of Parliament, as that they are not at all a compleat

Court,

Court, neither can they so unite or conioyne as to be an entire Court of either soveraigne or ministeriall iurisdiction. But are two distinct Courts (if so be the House of Commons which cannot minister an Oath, nor fine, nor imprison any but their own Members) may be called a Court, then are they Courts, not otherwise co-operating, than by concurrence of Votes in their severall Houses, for preparing matters in order to an Act of all the three Orders of the Parliament, which when they have done their Votes, are so farre from having any Legall Authoritie in the State, as that in Law there is no stile, nor forme of their joynt Acts, nor doth the Law so much as take notice of them, untill they have the royall assent, which if the King refuses, he yet doth no injurie to any, for that every of the three Orders that are the formall parts of the high Court of Parliament, (that is, the King, the Peeres, and Commons) are every of them by Law trusted for their own respective interests to be the onely assured Conservatours of the rights that do belong unto them, and may therefore every one of them freely dissent from the Votes of the other two, nor is their any danger that it should be so, but contrarily the most assured safetie that may be, for the consequence of their not agreeing can be no worse, than that their severall interests shall still remain in the condition that they were before, untill such time as that they shall all three agree upon the state of alteration. Now when the two Houses alone do no way make an entire Bodie, House, or Court, and when their is no known stile, nor forme of any Law, or Edict by the Votes of them two onely, nor any notice of them taken by the Law, it is apparant there is no Soveraignitie in their two Votes alone.

To argue now as some do, that the King must not deny His Vote, for if by denying it He may frustrate the Votes of the two Houses, by the same reason may He frustrate the Votes of all inferiour Courts, and open a way to the most boundlesse tyrannie that ever was, is a most perverse and absurde falsitie; there being no affinitie nor resemblance of the course of those

Courts with that of Parliament. For in inferiour Courts the Judges fit and give Judgement for the King, and not for themselves; and the Law there authorises them to give the Kings Judgement, and none but them, and therefore the Kings Diffent or Countermand cannot fruftrate their Judgements. But in Parliament the Peeres and Commons neither fit nor Vote for the King, but for themfelves. And the Law appoints the King himfelfe to give His own Vote there (which if the Peeres and Commons in His abfence could have fupplied, the Statute 33. H. 8. 21. needed not have provided that His Confent or Vote by His Letters under His Great Seale fhould be as effectuall, as if He himfelfe in Perfon had affented.) Befides the Judgement given by the Judges in inferiour Courts, is compleat in Law without the affent of the King, and therefore cannot be fruftrate by the Kings diffent; but the Votes of the two Houfes are therefore to be fruftrated for want of the Kings affent, becaufe without it they are not compleat nor perfect. The high Court of Parliament therefore refembling a Chaire of three feet, the two Houfes make but two of the three, which without the third is lame and ufeleffe (as to making of Law) but with the third becomes a firme and ufefull feate, and makes that facred *Tripos* from whence the Civil Oracles of our Law are delivered. When therefore we fpeake of the Soveraigne power and Authoritie of the Parliament, that never is to be underftood of the power of the two Houfes onely, nor any fuch Soveraigne power to be afcribed unto them.

Now in the laft place, we ufe the word Parliament for the three Orders of Parliament agreeing in their Votes; then, and then onely ufe we the word Parliament properly, and in that fenfe onely is the Parliament the fupreme Court, the higheft judicatorie, and moft foveraigne power, and authoritie in the Kingdom. But we muft ever underftand, that it is not the moft Soveraigne Court, for any Soveraignitie placed in the two Houfes, and from them transferred or communicated to His Majeftie, by their joyning or confenting with him; but it is

there-

therefore the most soveraigne Court, becaufe every compleat and perfect Act of it is the Act of the perfonall will, and power of the Soveraigne himfelfe, *Standing in His higheft Eftate Royall,* and (through the concurrence of thofe that are the inftrumentals of His reftraint) more freely and abfolutely working there, than in any other time and place he can do. For as a man that yeildeth himfelfe to be bound by keepers, hath the ufe of his ftrength taken from him, but none of the naturall ftrength it felfe, much leffe any of it transferred to them that bound him, but whenfoever they loofe his bonds, he again workes and acts by virtue of his own naturall ftrength, and not by any received from them: So the naturall right and intereft of the Soveraignitie being foly in the King, and the Peeres and Commons being onely intereffed in the Office of reftraining, for the regular working of true legitimate Soveraignitie, in whatfoever the Peeres and Commons by confenting remit the reftraint, the King in that willeth and worketh abfolutely by the power of his own inherent Soveraignitie. And whatfoever Act of the Court fo paffeth the hands of all the three Orders, does in truth virtually proceed from the King, as from the true and proper efficient thereof: which does not obfcurely nor rarely appear in our Acts of Parliament, but plainly and frequently throughout the whole Bodie of our ancient Lawes, *The King Willeth, the King Commandeth, the King Ordaineth, Provideth, Eftablifheth, Granteth, &c.* And yet though properly they be the Acts of the King in Parliament; yet are they alfo truly the Acts of the whole high Court of Parliament, becaufe that every of the three Eftates contribute their power according to the diverfitie of their office and intereft, the two Houfes by remitting through the confenting the reftraint, and the King by ufing his then unreftrained power.

Crompt. Iur. 10 *b.*
The fpeech of *H.* 8. in Parl. by information of the Judges.

Stat. Weft. 1, 3. *E.* 1.
1. 3. *E.* 1. 3.
& 6. &
42. *St at*, of Merch. 13. *E.* 1. *Weftm.* 3. 18. *E.* 1. *Stat. of Wafte* 20. *E.* 1. of Appeales, 18. *E.* 1. 1. *E.* 2. 1. and all the Titles of the Acts of our Parliament.

We are alfo to confider, that though this high Court of the three Orders be the fupreme Judicatorie of the Kingdome, yet it hath not that fuperioritie of judgement afcribed to it, for any foveraigne facultie it hath in difcerning the true dictate and refult

(11)

Unicuique in sua arte credendum, 11.H.7.9. 34.N.6.14.

sult of Law, no more than of any other particular Science (as of Divinitie, Philosophie, Physicke, Mathematiques, &c.) for the judgement of Sciences belongeth to the professours thereof, and the judgement of Law as well as of other Sciences. But the high Court of Parliament is the supreme judge, for the great trust the Law reposeth in the concurrence of all the three Orders, (who have meanes to have the best information of Law that the whole profession doth afford, and are supposed to use it) and likewise for the great power they have to binde all other judgement, and to make their sentence Law, though (as we have said) it were not Law before.

But we are further to observe that in the point of making of Law, the Law restraining thus the Soveraigne power to the consent of the *Peeres* and *Commons*, the more that by this regulation it purged it from destructive exorbitances, the more tender it grew of the just and legitimate rights thereof remaining, and therefore considering the person of the Soveraigne to be single, and his power counterpoised by the opposed wisedome of the two numerous Bodies of the two Houses, it al-

25.E.3.4. 37.E.3.13. 42.E.3.3. 17.R.2. *Vide the Oath of the Justices, an. 18 E.3.* Yee shall swear &c. that lawfully ye shall counsell the King in his businesse, and ye shall not

lowed unto the King power to sweare unto himselfe a Bodie of Councell of State (which our Lawes sometime call *His Grand Councell*) and to sweare unto him also Counsellours at Law, even the Judges themselves, and others learned in the Law, faithfully to advise him in his Government, that he may neither do nor receive wrong, especially not in Parliament, where the wrong may be perpetuall. And if upon a generall pretence of evill counsell, without any instance in what, his Majestie be deprived of the use and assistance of and assistance of any of his sworne Counsell (especially in Parliament time, when the Soveraignitie may be so easily overmatched) it will make such a breach of the priviledge of the first of the three Orders in Parliament, as will destroy the true frame of Parliaments, dimi-

counsell nor assent to any thing which may turne him in damage, &c. and ye shall do and procure the profit of the King, and of his Crown, with all things, where ye may reasonably do the same, and if ye be found in default, &c. ye shall be at the Kings will, of bodie, goods, and lands, thereof to do as shall please him. So helpe, &c. *Vide* the Statute *de Bigamis.*

nish

with the power of the Crown, and bring the settled estate of the Kingdome into the calamitous innovation of an unsettled and ever changing Forme of Government, and so into all manner of miserie and confusion.

The Soveraignitie in the King alone, is so clearly acknowledged by our Law, as that (unlesse we would reiect the iudgement and recognition of all our Parliament, and especially of all our most sincere and unquestioned Parliaments all the time of Queen *Elizabeth*, and ever since, all which do not onely affirme but (weare it) it would be idle to go about to make praise of it. But when the incredible perverseneffe of some, and in particular of him that writes, *The treacherie and disloyaltie of Papists, &c.* does not onely affirme the contrary, but would pretend to prove it. It cannot be a digression in a word or two to give some answer to his reasonings.

I shall passe over *Minshaw's* Dictionarie, *Speed, Stowe, Vowell, Foxe*, and others, whose authoritie he is not ashamed to cite for determining matter in Law, and which (if indeed it were a question) were of the greatest consequence that ever was stirred in Law. And because he so much insists upon *Bracton*, I shall briefly examine *Bracton*, and the Authours integritie in citing him and others.

And first, that all men may know how little authoritie in Law *Bracton* either now hath, or anciently hath had. Our yearebookes tell us that in the 35.H.6. It was declared by the whole Court, that *Bracton was never held an Authour in our Law*, and then it is not materiall what is the opinion of one that is of no authoritie. But if he were; yet those words in *Bracton* so much insisted on, *Rex habet superiorem Deum, Legem, item Curiam suam, &c.* are not indeed *Bractons* assertion. For *Bracton* speaking of the Kings Deeds and Charters, and affirming (which we would be loath should be Law at this day) that *Neither the Iustices nor private men may dispute the Kings Deed*, but that *if there be doubt of his Deed*, or Charter, *the resolution must come from the Kings own interpretation and will, &c.* Then goes he

35.H.6.
Fitz.Alr.
tit.gard.
72.*pag*.3
*Bract.li.*1
*c.*16.*par:*3
*fol.*34.

he on thus; *But some may say* (faith he) *that the King may do justice, and well: and if so, he may by the same reason do ill, and so put a necessitie upon him, that he mend the injurie, least both King and Iustices fall into the judgement of the living God for the injurie.* The King hath a Superiour, to wit, God: also the Law, by which he is made King: also His Court, to wit, the Earles and Barons, &c. Now whofoever confiders the place, it is all a reafoning which *Bracton* fuppofes fome other to make, and no affirmation of his own, and that is alfo plain by his words in another place, where fpeaking of the King, *If Iustice* (faith he) *be demanded of him, seing no Writ lies against him, one must petition, that he would correct and amend what he had done. Which if he do not, it is sufficient for his punishment, that he must expect God to be the Avenger of it.* Not a word of the Courts avenging or rectifying of the iniurie, or of their enforcing the King to do it himfelfe. Again, fpeaking of Earles, though with little iudgement he would feem to derive their Office from the Etymologie of the Latine name *Comes* (which was but a late borrowed tranflation brought in ufe by the Conquerour) and would fo make them a kinde of Companions with the King; yet does he not make them Companions thruft upon the King by Law, but *the Kings* (faith he) *do associate such to themselves for advice and government. Every one truly is under him, and he under none but God, and he hath no Peer in his Kingdom, for then he should loose the Command, when as one Peer hath no command over another, much lesse hath any one command over his superiour, (or so he should be inferiour to his own Subjects: and the King ought not to be under man, but under God, and the Law:* now thefe words of *Bracton* tell us that the other are neither his affertion nor approbation.

And whereas by thofe words of *Bracton*, that *The King ought to be under the Law*, he would inferre a direct Soveraignitie over the King, he very much corrupts the meaning of *Bracton*, for it is one thing to be fubiect to Law, and to the adminiftration of Law, and another thing to be a Subiect to thofe that have the adminiftration of Law as to his Soveraignes. Our Saviour Chrift

B.ad.li.1. c.8 p.5.

Chrift was fubject to the Law, and to the adminiftration of the Law in the hands of them that were the Minifters of it: yet was not *Chrift* the Subject of thofe Minifters, nor they his Soveraignes, but contrary he theirs, he being *Borne King of the Iewes*. And *Bracton's* reafon that the King muft be under the Law is, *becaufe he is Chrifts Vicar on earth*. And *Chrift* himfelfe was under the Law; fo as plainly *Bracton* meanes not the King, otherwife under the Law, then as our Saviour *Chrift* was, who did fubject himfelfe to the juft execution of the pofitive Lawes of the Kingdom, of which he himfelfe was the Head and Fountain, not that he fhould be fubject to the adminiftration of any arbitrary Law, refiding in the people, who fhould in the laft refort be Soveraignes over their own King: for that was not futable to one that fhould be *Vicar of Chrift*, but to a *Vicar of the people*. Neither is the King more fubject to any judgement that can be given in Parliament, than He is to judgements given in inferiour Courts, to which if you will fay the Parliament is fuperiour to thofe Courts, and the fuperioritie that is but fubordinately in them is foveraignely in the Parliament; truly the fuperioritie (if it may fo be call'd) that is fubordinately in the inferiour Courts, is but more fuperiourly in the Houfe of Lords than them, but it is not foveraignely neither in the Lords Houfe, nor any other part of Parliament, till we come to the judgement of all the three Eftates, (where the Kings will is the efficient formall of the Law) and there you may fee that the Vicar of *Chrift* the King, like *Chrift* His Lord, whom He reprefenteth; in being fubject to the Law, of which He is Soveraigne, becomes at laft fubject to none but Himfelfe: for that high Court of Parliament fpeaketh not without Him.

But ere we give over his citation of *Bracton*, we muft not forget his unfaithfull application of it. For as for thofe words, *The King hath a fuperior* (that is to fay) *God, alfo the Law, alfo His Court, to wit, the Earles and Barons*. He would not onely have them *Bracton's* words, and have them underftood to carry Soveraignitie over the King, but would have that Soveraignitie placed in the two Houses, when as *Bracton* expresly expounds that the Court which he meanes is the *Earles and Barons*, that is to say, the House of Lords onely, and not the Commons too, plainly shewing that he meanes no other superioritie than such as is incident to the regular course of Justice in the way of legall suit and processe, which in that course never goes further than the House of Lords: there is no forme of prosecution in that kinde in the two Houses, and therefore neither Soveraignitie nor Superioritie in that kinde can be ascribed to them.

Pag.38. Neither may we passe over his falshood and shuffling to extenuate the Oath of Supremacie, that securitie may make men swallow their perjurie and never know it: for though it be true, that the Oath was pricipally intended againft Papacie, (because the *Papacie* was the first that ever pretended Soveraignitie over Kings) and the clause of renouncing runnes against Forraigne powers onely, as those that then were onely feared to be pretenders under the Papacie; yet the recognition it selfe, that *The King is the onely Supreme Governour*. And the Oath it selfe, to *beare faith and true Alleageance to the King, His Heires, and Successours, and to assist and defend all jurisdictions, priviledges, preheminences, and authoritie belonging to them, &c.* are clearly generall, absolute, and unrestrained to any particularitie of *P*apacie, Forraigners, or any thing else whatsoever.

But to come to that that is the maine Authoritie, scope, and drift of his book, and which he would by all meanes inculcate though but under the shew of telling what popish Parliaments have done, lest otherwise his horrible intention might appear, he brings us precedents that the two Houses of Parliament have upon all occasion soveraignely disposed of the Crown, and of all the rights that do belong unto it, and that even our Kings themselves have submitted their soveraigne rights to the determination of the two Houses. Good God! How *Evill men and Seducers wax worse and worse, deceiving, and being deceived.* He that writ the Observations upon His Maiesties Answers and Expresses had so much ingenuitie left him as to acknowledge,

2 Tim. 3.13.

that

that *There was never King depofed by any Parliament lawfully affem-bled*; and that the Acts of the Parliament, *R.2.* were not so properly the Acts of the two Houfes as of *H.*4. and His victorious Armie. But this man being not afhamed to licke up what his fellow vomited out, prefents the world with a cull of all the irregular times of our unfortunate Princes, in which (by the confent of all men) the Acts of neither fide are to be drawn into example, and bring us for judiciall Authorities, the horrid facts of irregular power, in the Times of King *Iohn, R.2. H.4. H 6. &c.* And is fo supine in his purpofe, that with the factious Parliaments in the Times of *H.3. E 2.* and *R.2.* (which he cites to have exercifed authoritie over Kings) he ftickes not to couple the Rebellions in the North, againft *H.4.* and the rebellious Infurrections of *Iacke Cade, Iacke Straw, Wat Tyler*, Doctour *Mackerell, Ket*, and others, as Acts that made equall proofe of the foveraigne power of the Peeres and Commons: indeed in both there were much what the fame pretences, and both had much what the fame warrant. *Ed.2. Pag.8. to pag.15. pag. 15.*

But all thofe Parliaments as they were called in the troublefome Times of Faction, and Civill War, fo were they ever fwayed by thofe that were the Heads of the moft potent Faction, and while they alwayes acted in favour of them and their Defigne, they are fo farre from being inftances of the power, and authoritie of the two Houfes, as that cleane contrary, they are plain inftances of the weakneffe and unfteadineffe of them; when forfaking the moderation and guidance of their naturall Head, they fuffered themfelves to be lead by the private conduct of every popular pretender; and fo even among the precedents which he citeth, we fee that when *Canutus* prevailed by his Armes, he could have a Parliament refolve that his Title was the beft. When *Hen.*4. had an Armie of 60000. he could have a Parliament depofe *R.2.* and conferre the Crown upon himfelfe. When *Edw.* Duke of *Yorke* grew potent, he could have a Parliament be the inftrument of determining the Raigne of *H.*6. and leave him onely the name of King for his life, *Pag.33, 34,35,35.*

(18)

but give the Duke the very Kingdom, under the names of *Protectour* and *Regent*, *Edw*.4. could by Parliament procure *H* 4. *H*.5. & *H*.6. to be declared Kings in fact, but not in right: *R*.3. though an Usurper, could procure a Parliament to declare him a lawfull King. *Henry* 7. could procure the forementioned Acts in favour of *Edw*.4. & *R*.3. to be adnulled. *Hen*.8. could have a Parliament authorise his Divorces. And Queen *Elizab*. could by Parliament make it High Treason to say, that the Queen could not by Act of Parliament binde and dispose the rights and Titles which any person whatsoever might have to the Crown; when yet we know that no Act of Parliament, no not an Attainder by Parliament, can disable the right Heire to the Crown, because the descent of the Crown upon Him purges all disabilities whatsoever, and makes Him capable of it.

[margin: Parliament knot jurisdiction nor ownRight. Adjudged H.7.]

This is the summe and true estimate of all the Authorities which he cites, in which if the Acts could be granted to be the meer Acts of the two Houses; yet did they no more prove the soveraigne power to be in the two Houses, than the Popes deposing of Kings proves the right of deposing them to be in him, that the things were done, is no proofe that they were lawfully done: and yet as idle and vile a collection of examples (not to be imitated) as he hath made, he is fain to belie them to makem seem to serve his turne; for truly though he affirmes that the popish Parliaments, &c challenged, or claimed, greater jurisdiction over Kings, than any ever since, yet his instances prove no more claime of Soveraignitie than a robber claimes when he exercises an arbitrary power over a mans person and fortunes: what they did they did *de facto*, upon some inferiour reasons, not upon claime of the Soveraignitie; they neither taught, nor ever learn'd that Jesuitique *depth of Sathan*, that the Soveraignitie over the Soveraigne is placed in the Bodie Representative of the Subject. All claime therefore of either the Soveraignitie it selfe, or of the rights thereof by any Representative of the Subject, is a transcendent impietie beyond the parallell of all his unimitable examples, in which I cannot

[margin: Pag. 4.]

(19)

cannot but the more wonder that he should ascribe the Acts unto the two Houses, when by making the Acts theirs, he makes all the long miserie and bloodshed that ensued upon those Acts to have been brought upon the Land by the meer Act of the two Houses. Considering therefore the every way faulty Argument of that Book, both in citing and applying, I am forced to conclude with the same words that in the frontispice of his Book he begins with *The treacherous dealers have dealt treacheronsly; yea, the treacherous dealers have dealt exceeding treacherously.*

As for the second part of the same Author that came since forth under a title that pretends to shew the *Lawfulnes of a defensive war;* that answers it selfe, that it comes nothing to the case in question, where the War is acknowledged to be an Invasive War to take from His Majestie certain Counsellours, pretended to be evil Counsellours. If possibly therefore he should prove what he undertakes to maintain that Subjects may make a Defensive War against their Soveraigne, yet being nothing to our case deserves at all no answer here, I therefore returne again unto my purpose.

That the Soveraignitie (with all the rights claimed by His Majestie) is in the King inseparably inherent in the person of His Majestie; we have not onely the forementioned testimonies and reasons, but we have the witnesse of the two Houses themselves, for whom our deceiving Pamphlets do now make all the new arguments of pretence. For first, we have (as I have said) the whole current and bodie of our very Acts of Parliament acknowledging it in these very termes, *Our Soveraigne Lord the King.* We have the Parliament 25. H.8 declaring thus, *This Your Graces Realme recognizing no Superiour under God but Your Grace.* The Parliament 16. R. 2. 5. affirming *The Crown of England hath been so free at all times, that it hath been in no earthly subjection, but immediately to God, in all things touching the regalitie of the said Crown, and to none other.* In the 25. H. 5. both Houses declare *That it belongeth to the Kings regalitie to grant or denie what petitions in Parliament he pleaseth.* In the 15. E. 3. The King being unwillingly drawn to consent to certain Articles prejudiciall

Co. 5. de Jure & Eccl. fol. 9. b.

25 H. 8.
21.
16. R. 2. 5.
25. H. 5.
15. E. 3.

to the Crown, and to promise to seale the Statute thereupon made, least otherwise his affaires in hand might have been ruinated. Another Statute the same year reciting the matter enacted in these words, *It seemed to the said Earles, Barons, and otherwise men, that since the Statute did not of Our free will proceed, the same be void, and ought not to have the name nor strength of a Statute, and therefore by their counsaile and assent We have decreed the said Statute to be void, &c.* In the Statute of Banishment of *H. Spencer*, the first Article against him, is for making a Bill, wherein he affirmed *Homage and alleageance to the King is more by reason of their own, than of the person of the King.* The word hath a note of a Parliament roll Diarie of *H.4*. The Commons in Parliament pray the King that *They may not be made parties to any judgement in Parliament, but where in rei veritate they are parties, for that the judgement belongs onely to the King, except where it is given by Statute.* As for the *Militia*, the Shippes and Forts of the Kingdom. The King and His Predecessours have not onely been ever in possession of them, commanded and disposed of them even during the sitting of Parliaments, but have enjoyed that possession without any claime of right made by the two Houses, and our Law hath not a surer badge of right than continuall and unquestioned possession. Besides, the Parliament it selfe, *7.E.1.* declares unto the King, that *To him of right belongs straightly to defend* (that is, to forbid) *all force of Armes, and thereunto they are bound to assist him as their Soveraigne Lord.* The Statute *11.H.7 18.* reciteth, *Where every Subject by the dutie of his Alleageance is bound to serve assist his Prince and Soveraigne Lord at all seasons when need shall require, &c.* In the 3. of *Edw.3.* The House of Commons disclaime the having cognizance of such matters, as the guarding of the Seas and Marches of the Kingdom. And by the Statute *25.E.3.2.* It is made High Treason for any to meddle with the *Militia*, so farre as *To levie Warre against the King, or to aide them that do it.* And we all know that to levie Warre without Commission from the King, or to give aide unto it, is by our Law to levie War, and give aide *against our Sove-*

Soveraigne Lord the King, His Crown and Dignitie. And we never knew of any exception out of that Law in case the Werre were levied by Authoritie of the two Houses? And when we have not in our power to search the Parliament rols for clearing these things. If (besides our published Statutes) our Law-bookes have any authoritie, we have not onely *Bracton* (whom they insist upon) but other authentique Law-bookes concurring with him who all speaking of the King and the Houses do expresly say, that seeing *The King hath no Peere, The King cannot be iudged by them*. So that whatsoever authoritie is in the constant practice of the Kingdom, and whatsoever authoritie in the known and published Lawes and Statutes, all do conclude the Soveraignitie in the person of the King, and the alleageance, faith, obedience of the Subject even of the Subject virtually united in the Bodie Representative, to be inevitably devinct and obliged to the person of the King.

3.*E*.3. *Fitz, tit. Cor. Bam. pl Cor.* 153. *Bract,li 2. cap 22 fol.* 52.4 *Rex parem non habet, nec vicinum nec superiorem.*

The Soveraignitie both of the frame of the State and positive Lawes of the Kingdome being fixed in the person of the King, and the Alleageance of the Subject by Law inevitably thither assigned, then comes in Religion, and fortifies, and enforces all those bonds of dutie and obedience, and that under the severe menace of damnation, which when it is in divers precepts and examples (well known unto us) abundantly set forth in the Scriptures. It will not be safe for us to let slip the consideration of two examples especially.

The Children of *Israel* being redeemed out of *Egypt*, baptized in the Red Sea, and brought for triall into the wildernesse as they were the type of the Church of God in all Kingdomes whatsoever in this world: so *Moses* their Governour was the type of that regall power under which the Church of God in this world was generally to be governed: so as though he were not a King in point of interest, (for the people were not yet in the Countrey that was to be the Kingdom, neither was *Moses* of the Tribe to whom the Kingdom was promised) yet (saith the Text) *He was King when the heads of the people were assembled*. *Deut. Moses* 33.5.

Moses so personating the kingly Office, when as yet there was no expresse command concerning obedience and subjection, more than *Honour thy father and thy mother, and he that curseth father or mother let him die the death.* It happened that *Corah, Dathan,* and *Abiram* rebelled against him, and their rebellion was but this: they in the behalfe of the Congregation of the Lord, because that it *was holy every one of them, and the Lord among them,* question *Moses* his Soveraignitie, charge him and *Aaron* that they exalted themselves above the Congregation of the Lord, and that *Moses* had not kept touch with them to bring them to a Land that flowed with milke and honey, but sought to starve them in the wildernesse, while blinding the eyes of the people he might in the mean time make himselfe a Prince over them, and out of jealousie of this they refused obedience to *Moses,* and would not come at him when he sent to call them, and so much was their cause believed to be just and right: as that they were seconded with *two hundred and fifty Princes of the Assemblie famous in the Congregation :* all of them so confident, that they durst joyne issue with *Moses,* and put themselves upon triall by Gods immediate judgement in the case, and they were also backed with many thousands of the people. This was the Rebellion: the Judgement we all know to be most exemplar Judgement that ever was given in any case. The Heads of the Rebellion *Corah, Dathan,* and *Abiram,* with their wives, their children, and all their substance, were swallowed up of the earth, they *went down quicke into Hell* (saith the Psalmist.) The two hundred and fifty that invaded the holy Office were slain with fire from Heaven, and fourteen thousand and seven hundred of the people (that favoured their attempts and murmured at the Judgement) were in an instant (in lesse than *Aaron* could get his Censer with fire from the Altar and run among them) consumed in a speedy plague.

It will be objected that *Moses* was a man of extraordinary calling, and that Rebellion against an ordinary Governour (though a soveraigne King) is not like Rebellion against a Governour

Numb. 16.3.

ib.v.13.

ib.v.2.

Psal. 106. 17.

vernour of so extraordinary calling and priviledge; all that granted, yet this exemplar Judgement comes home to manifest the hainous sin of rebelling against Kings at this day.

Moses had an extraordinary calling, he could not else have been a type of regal Authoritie, but in type *He was King when the heads of the people were assembled.* He had the Priest made subordinate to him, *He shall be unto thee instead of a mouth, and thou shalt be unto him instead of God.* And had the Magistracie, derived from his Authoritie, to beare the burthen with him, *God took off the spirit that was upon him, and put it upon the seventie two Elders.* So *Moses* was clearly endued with regall power; and for trangression against that very Authoritie of his was the Judgement made so exemplar. It could not be exemplar in regard of any other Authoritie which he had then, and no other since either had or could have: but that we may know the Judgement was exemplar against Rebellion, against regall Dominion, which would often be committed in the later dayes, the holy Ghost speaking against the seducers & deceivers wch in *the later dayes* should make *perilous times,* describes them not onely by being *Cursed speakers, disobedient to parents*; (that is, as well to Civil parents as Natural) *traiterous, headie, high-minded, resisting the truth:* like them that resisted *Moses; Despising Dominion, despising Government, speaking evill of Dignities, of those that are in Authoritie, of those things which they know not, &c.* but by this likewise that *They perish in the gainsaying of Corah.* The other example is that of *David.* Saul was a wicked apostate King, from whom *The Spirit of God* (the inward anointing) *was departed. Saul rejected from raigning over Israel.* So by God himselfe declared. *David* in his stead by *God provided to be King:* and to that end by Gods command anointed; by all which *David's* priviledge then was more above the priviledge of all Subjects now, than *Saul's* priviledge of that time was above the priviledge of Kings at this day; and yet *David* for all those circumstances so much authorising him, and dis-authorising *Saul,* did not know *Who could lay his hands upon the Lords Anointed and be guiltlesse.* Nay, he did but lay his hand upon

Deut. 33.5.
Exo. 4.16.
Numb. 11.15.
2 Tim. 3.
2. & 4.
2 Pet. 2.10
Jude 8.
10. & 11.
1 Sam. 16.14. verse 1.
1 Sam. 26.9.

D   Saul's

Afterward David was touched in heart because he had cut off the lap of Sauls garment.
2 Sam. 24.6.

Saul's garment to cut off the lap for a testimonie of his loyaltie, and innocent intention toward *Saul,* and yet even for that (saith the Text) *his heart smote him* ; that he cried out, *The Lord forbid I should do that thing to my Master, to lay mine hand upon the Lords Anointed :* his reason we may know in the other words of his, *The Lord shall smite him, or his day shall come to die, or he shall descend into battaile, and perish: the Lord keep me from laying mine hand upon him :* plainly inferring, that to call Princes to account belongs onely to God : that God hath time and wayes of his own to do it in, and will do it : and that therefore man must not meddle with the doing of it : for if anointed *David* might not intermeddle with rejected *Saul,* much lesse may common Subjects meddle with their unrejected Soveraignes. Sufficiently therefore do these examples shew the heinousnesse of Subiects lifting up themselves, and resisting the person of their Soveraigne, upon what pretence soever.

Now while the severitie of these examples, and other passages of Scripture, iustly striking terrour into every soule, does make us wonder what great straight of humane affaires could be so violent an impulsive with us, as to make Christian Subiects contrary to sworne Faith, to Law, and to Religion, not onely disobey their Soveraigne, but resist, invade the soveraigne rights, and imploy their Soveraignes *Militia,* Shippes, Forts, Armes, Treasure, yea and his own sworne Subiects too against Him ; truly all that the most searching thought can finde to secure his conscience with, against the horrour of so foule a guilt, is, that otherwise we feare (or pretend to feare) that His Maiestie, seduced by evill Counsellours, by popishly affected Prelates, Courtiers, and Cavaliers, should destroy our Law, our Parliaments, our established Forme of Government, and change them into tyrannnie, and the true Protestant Religion into Poperie. This, this Feare or pretence of Fear alone is all the warrant we can finde for our unparallelled proceedings against our Soveraigne. And if this before the Tribunall of God, and of our own Lawes be not sufficient for our excuse, then have we

no-

nothing to discharge us of the guilt of publique violence, robberie, murder, periurie, treason, resistance of the Ordinance of God, and of forcing others against their consciences by act or aid to resist with us. Now all these evils are universally committed all over the Kingdome, and all these evils upon no other warrant done, than that the good of Reformation (as is pretended) may come thereon. So make we the Word of God of none effect, while we entertain and preferre the Jesuitique tradition before it, and maintain that what is for the good of the Church must be done, notwithstanding any bonds of dutie, of Faith, or Oath whatsoever to the contrary.

And if we examine the grounds of this Feare, and what iust suspition and probabilitie of such an innovation, as is pretended to be feared, is given. We see for our assurance to the contrary, that His Maiestie (after once He was truly informed of our grievances) condescended not onely to give us ease of them, but to make His Acts of Grace in them at once exceed the Acts of all His Predecessours since the granting of our *Magna Charta*; and did not onely in present relieve our sufferings, but (often invoking the Sacred Maiestie of God, as a severe Witnesse of His purpose for the time to come) tie Himselfe for ever to settle matters of Religion according to the purest times of the Protestant Church of *England* (with such ease for tender Consciences, as by a lawfull iudgement of the Clergie should be iudged fit) and to governe according to the known Lawes of the Land. Here is little signe of one led by evill counsaile, or of a minde that would subdue Law & Religion to the satisfaction of His private will. This shewes our Fear to be both groundles and wicked; and indeed, after this if iealousie it selfe could yet make scruple of any thing, how easie were it for the wisdome of the Bodie Representative, by preparing a Law of severitie against the instruments of innovation, exposing their persons and fortunes to certain ruine, nullifying the innovations themselves, and discharging the Subiect from all obedience and conformitie unto them, to have secured the Kingdom against all manner of fear in that kinde, when as His Majeſtie freely offers His Gracious aſſent to any Act that ſhould in that behalfe be neceſſary.

But (if what cauſe, what ground, what reaſon of dutie ſoever we finde, though conſtantly and univerſally received for true, both by the judgement of our Law, and by the authoritie of our Religion, we muſt notwithſtanding reject all to believe the all-concluding judgement of the Bodie Repreſentative, whom we never knew to have ſuch Supremacie of iudgement, till it ſelfe bearing witneſſe of it ſelfe did tell us ſo) it cannot yet but make much to the ſatisfaction of the conſcience, to examine how well the two Houſes, now ſitting, do attain the condition of a full and free Aſſemblie of the two Houſes of Parliament, that pretend to have ſuch iudgement.

And firſt it is known that the Houſe of Commons now ſitting, however elected, was never yet perfected by a right determination of Elections, but that ſome ſet as Members there that ought not to have been returned, and ſome are not received that yet were rightly choſen, ſome are excluded for having hands in Monopolies, and proiects; and others (as much intereſſed in them) for their aſſured affection reteined: the greateſt part of both Houſes, by meanes of popular menacings, tumults, poaſting up of names, branding men with the name of Malignants, (things never known before in Parliaments) and again undeſerved expellings from the Houſe, or impriſonings, have been ſo over-awed, that they have been forced to ſuppreſſe their Votes, to give them contrary to their iudgements, to hide themſelves, or to flie from the Houſes; the reſidue of both Houſes, (and among them the Knights and Burgeſſes which the Countries ſent to reſide in Parliament, that there the whole Repreſentative adviſing together, might with the more ſafetie Vote and conſent for us) they make over their Countries truſt to a few Committees of their own, and wholly betake themſelves to martiall Offices and imployments, exerciſing in them a new found arbitrary power over thoſe that ſent them. And then the remainder of the Peeres and Commons (which are

ſcarce

scarce a fourth part of them) call themselves the Parliament, and all the known rights of Soveraignitie does this Epitome of Parliament assume unto themselves and exercise; yea, the House of Commons alone (notwithstanding their Protestation to God for the Defence of the Lawes and Libertie of the Subject) by warrant under their Speakers hand, beyond all Law and example, imprison Subjects, that were never Members of their House, and deny them their *Habeas Corpus*. And not onely invade the Libertie of the Commons, but presse upon the House of Lords, the voting of things which in a full House they had before, upon mature advice, orderly rejected. They seconded a tumultuous Petition that demanded the names of the Lords that had dissented from the Commons House, though the dissenters were the *major* part of the House of Lords. This Epitome of Parliament hath taught that which never Parliament knew before, That their Members may not without the Order of their House be restrained, no not for Treason. And, professing tender care of the Kings Honour and safetie, hath authorised Bookes, wherein His Soveraignitie is made subject to the Representative of His Subiects, and wherein the deposing of our English Kings by their Subiects is declared warrantable; and upon the authoritie and warrant of this Parliament must the poor Christian Subiect that is under their power (against his Conscience) act and give aide to the Armie, which against the Kings expresse Command and Proclamations they have levied; when though conscious horrour and shame will not suffer it to be acknowledged to be raised against the King, yet are their Souldiers sure they shall meet with no other opposite than with their rightfull Soveraigne, and His Followers arming for the safetie of His Person, for defence of the iust rights of the Crown, for the due Priviledges of the first of the three Orders of Parliament, and for the necessary power wherewith He is to protect Religion, Lawes, and Subiects of His Kingdom. Who that makes conscience of what he does, as one that must make account for it before the

The Book of Observations, Treacheries and disloyalties of Papists, &c.

great

great Tribunal (where a little integritie (though now despised) and a little innocence of cause shall bring one more support than either King on the one side, or Parliament on the other, or Armie on either side) who (I say) thereof mindfull, can against the thousand witnesses of his conscience, recede from the dutie which all his life, till now, hath both by Law and Christian Religion been inculcate to him, and rejecting all, cast himselfe soule, bodie, and fortunes, wholly upon the new-found warrant of strangely conditioned apparition of Parliament.

These, and other particulars that may be instanced in, take off the confidence and repose that one would otherwise have in the two Houses, especially when they (setting on foot claimes and pretences, not agreeing with the dutie that men from their youth have found their consciences ever bound unto) go not the faire and open way of satisfaction, to have in so high concernments the Parliament Rolls as freely and fully searched on the Kings behalfe, as on the Parliaments, and to have their new and strange learning, as freely argued by the Kings Councell, and by the Judges, as by the instruments of the Parliament: but as the Papacie, in invading the Soveraignitie of the Church, Voted her selfe into the Supremacie, and then suppressed all examination of the Truth by damning all Writings to the contrary, and branding the Authours and users of them with the name of Heretickes: So we invading the Soveraignitie of our own State, Vote our selves into it, brand with the name of Malignants, all that concurre not with us in it, interdict them the freedome of search and discoverie of the Truth, and damne their Writings as scandalous and seditious Pamphlets; and so making them Vote-convicted State Heretickes, We thenceforth hold no Faith nor Truth to be kept toward them, but prosecute them as Enemies to the State, for no other offence but because we have made them Malignants, popishly affected, dissolute, desperate, blood-sucking Cavaliers and plunderers.

Yet truly, if we consider the qualitie of them that adhere unto His Maiestie and to His Cause do now lie under that censure

sure, we shall finde them the flower and **greater part of our Nobilitie** and Gentrie of the Kingdome, **the greater part of His Majesties Honourable Privie Counsell**, yea and of **His Great Councell** too, even of the **Peeres and Commons**, the chiefe of the Judges, and with them the opinion of the residue even of that whole Profession, the spirits and prayers of the farre greatest part of the Clergie, and the hearts of the greater part of the most substantiall men of the Commonaltie, whose soule and conscience, presented with the consideration of these things, would not shrinke with inward horrour to thinke he should either attempt or give aide to the cutting off (not like *David*, of a lap of his Soveraignes ordinary garment) but of this lively apparrell-politique of his Soveraigne, wherewith for safetie, as well as ornament, His Majestie is now begirt; nay, to cut off the very limbes of his Civill bodie, and not without eminent danger to His Sacred Person, how loud and frightfull would the spirit of *David* crie in the eares of his guilty conscience, *The Lord forbid I should do this thing to lift up my hand against the Lords Anointed.*

O, but Religion is now at stake, and it is not to be believed that popishly affected Counsellours and Commanders with the helpe of a popish Armie should so much forsake their own ends as to fight for Establishment of the true Protestant Religion: truly it is sincerely confessed, it is not likely, and therefore I shall never believe that the Designe of Reforming our Religion by the hands of Brownists, Anabaptists, and Sectaries, (which by a constant and credible report, is believed to have been so much fostered and advanced by the Cardinall *Richelieu* and the late French Embassadour, as that *Chambers* the Cardinals Secretarie was on purpose sent into the *Scotish* Armie here in *England*) was ever with intent of Establishing the true Protestant Religion, or that for the Protestant Religions sake, the death of the Cardinall was by some of our active Parliament men (in our hearing) lamented as of a great friend of the Parliament, or that the great correspondence and intercourse observed

served to be between the late French Embassadour and Master *Pym*, was for the advancement of the Protestant Religion. But where is any popish Armie, under the conduct of popish Commanders, that, according to the Designe of popish Counsellours, is likely to oppresse the Protestants, and advance Poperie? Certainly, both his Maiestie, and his Protestant Followers are well assured, that not any part of the Warre is managed by the Designe of persons that are so affected; but who knowes not the ground of calumnie? The King must either denie his Subiects that are Papists the protection of his Armie, and refuse their aide and service, or else their aide and service must make his Armie a popish Armie: surely, not to admit them into his Armie, when they cannot otherwise be safe, were uniustly to deny them the protection of Subiects, and to spare them (either in their personall or pecuniarie assistance) were with inequalitie toward his Protestant Subiects, and with danger to their Cause, to refuse his needfull duties from the Papists: though therefore Protestants should never lay down their iealousie of the growth of Poperie, yet should they not let it so abuse them, as to make them believe they have no danger to feare but onely Poperie; especially now when Schisme and Sectarisme do with such authoritie invade us, and when nothing can more advance the bringing in of Poperie, if it be possible, than the confusion in Church and State that does inevitably follow them (the expectance whereof was the cause that made the Cardinall and the popish partie from beyond sea so effectually labour the promoting of them.) Undoubtedly, if Poperie be at this time to be feared, it is to be feared from the prevailing of Schismatickes by the Designe and manage of so potent and active forraigne Instruments of Poperie; and it would returne with comfortable satisfaction to our consciences, that having for a feigned feare of Poperie engaged our selves in reall Rebellion, we should finde our paines rewarded with the felicitie of becomming instruments of the evill that at so deare a rate we did unnecessarily resist.

When

When in every thing confiderable to refolution, the confcience is on every hand fo ftrongly befet with reafons, all concluding for obedience to our Soveraigne, and for our utmoft affiftance to His Caufe. How weak is the fole Authoritie of an imperfect reprefentative of Peeres and Commons, fo to poffeffe the confcience with perfwafion to the contrary, as upon it to venture the prefent and eternall fafetie of ones felfe, and of fo many thoufands in our *Ifrael*.

But fay that this world were onely to be confidered in the bufineffe, let us yet but fee what muft needs be the event, in cafe the Parliament Forces (which God forbid) fhould prevaile; either they muft leave the Soveraignitie in the King as it was before, and content themfelves with ftrict Lawes againft all grievances that may be feared in Religion or in Government: (and then they bring no more to paffe then what His Majeftie, before their Warre, did of himfelfe, and does yet gratioufly offer) or elfe they muft take the foveraigne power from the King into their own hands, and leave him no more (at moft) than the contemptible name of King, then fhall we loofe our old legall Government, and be governed by the abfolute arbitrary and tyrannicall way of their Votes, and they, to fecure themfelves in that new and uncouth way of Government that they muft inftitute, muft (to the overthrow of Trade, and intolerable burthen of the Subject) keep the Kingdome under perpetuall Garrifons; and then what with the Faction and difcord of our ambitious New-States, what with the unrulineffe of the commanding Souldier, and what with the attempts of thofe whofe fidelitie will ever excite their utmoft endeavour for their Soveraignes never dying right, we fhall fall into an inceffant Civill Warre, (untill the Kingdome being ruined) the Soveraignitie returne into the hand to which it rightfully belongeth.

Unles therefore it pleafe God, that our great *Metropolis* of *London* (partaking rather of the wife fpirit of the men of *Abel*, than of the obftinacie of *Gibeah* the *Benjamite*) fhall either deale fo 2 Sam. 20.16.

E effectually

effectually with those that there reside in shew of Parliament, as that they bring them to yield to the equalitie of a free and legall Parliament, and so provide against future grievances, without any violation of the Rights of the Crown: or else, (in case they refuse) shall like the *Abelites*, deliver unto the King
Judges 20 the Heads of those Oppofites that rise up against Him. We may assure our selves that that Citie like those of *Gibeah* and *Benjamin*, are hardened to all our *Israels* punishment, and to their own destruction, and may (as they did) prevaile once, and again, against the residue of the Kingdome, untill they have fulfilled Gods determined Visitation upon the Land, and then consummate all with their deplorable destruction.

FINIS.

A DISCOVERIE OF LONDONS OBSTINACIE, AND MISERIE.

Here hath been many Admonitions sent from His Majestie, advising that Citie of their own preservation, yet they have continued stubborne, though they cannot but see the hand of the Lord to assist all the King's Majesties proceedings, whereas their actions are so farre from prosperitie that they winde themselves wilfully, and force others ignorantly, into miserable adversitie.

Furthermore, *though* God hath manifestly fought *against* the Rebells *for* the *King*, giving Him Victorie in many Battailes, when all humane helpes and advantages were on the Rebells side, *though* God hath miraculously, and beyond the hope of man restored unto Him the *hearts* of the people, (which the Heads of this Rebellion by slander had stolne from Him:) *though* from small and contemptible beginnings in the eyes of

E 2 His

His Enemies (few or none ftanding for Him, but God and the juftice of His Caufe) God hath profpered him into many mighty Armies, which render Him formidable to the proudeft, and ftouteft of the Rebels, *though* every *Victorie* hath been feconded by a tender of *Peace*, and with an overture of *Pacification*, fo that as Himfelfe fpeakes in that Declaration publifhed *July* 30 1643. *He could not probably fall under the fcandalous imputation which hath ufually attended His Meſſages of Peace, that they proceed from the weakneſſe of His Power, not love of His People*. Laftly, *though* like an indulgent Father of rebellious Children, He hath *courted* this *Citie*, and *wooed* it, by many pardons, many, and often repeated Acts of Grace and Favour to recall us to our former Loyaltie, (if ever we were Loyall) yet, incohfiderate, unthankfull wretches as we are, we over-look, or fleight all thefe invitations, for inftead of returning, we have added this, as the complement of our other Rebellions, that (whether more unthankfully or undutifully, I cannot tel) we have caft dirt in our Soveraignes face, and flandered *the footfteps of Gods Anointed*; as if He were guiltie of all thofe Miferies, which at this time threaten the fubverfion of this Nation: we will no longer wound the King *fecretly*, through the fides of his evill *Counfellours*, or *Cavaliers*, but charge Him *directly, and point blanke*, as in that moft feditious Declaration, or whatever you will call it, prefented by Sir *David Watkins*, and that broken Citizen, out at elbowes, called *Satten Shute*, to the Common-Councell, and by them to the remainder of the *Lower Houſe*, if it be not breach of Priviledge to call it fo.

How willing have we obeyed every Commandment, except God and the Kings? *How forward* have we been to employ the large Revenues of our feverall Companies, and Brotherhoods, (as heretofore to exceffe, and gluttonie, fo now) to fupport this Rebellion? *How ready*, even beyond our abilities, have we been to fubmit to every *Taxe*, and *illegall Impoſition*, even to the bondage & flaverie of *Excife*. by which we are not fo much *Proprietaries* of our own, as *Stewards*, or *Cafheerers* to the heads

of

of the Rebellion, and all this, to no other end but to keep up the Rebellion: we have not onely protected, and supported the Kings *mortall Enemies*, but as much as in us lay, have persecuted all His *Friends*, or, if but suspected to stand well affected to Him, and the Justice of His Cause, not sparing the effusion of *innocent blood*, as that of Master *Tomkins*, and Master *Chaloner*, which, like the blood of *Abel*, calls loud to Heaven for vengeance, on this bloody Citie, and questionlesse will in time be heard, for not content to buy these mens bloods with great summes of monies, which could not be advanced but on this condition, that Master *Tomkins*, and Master *Chaloner*, be delivered up to their pleasure, and murthered for a strange *Conspiracie* called *Obedience* to the *King*, but being dead, in an unheard of barbarousnesse they presse into the houses, where their dead bodies lay, before their Funerals, and thinking they could never be *sure* enough of so great a *guilt*, they will not believe that they are dead, unlesse they force the houses to see the bodies of them whom themselves had murthered; insomuch, that to avoid further violence and rage of the Citizens, they were fain to set open the doores where their bodies lay, and expose them to the view of all, that so they might glut themselves with beholding that sad spectacle which themselves had made.

That the Kings Gracious offers of Peace have been slighted, and rejected, with scorne, and contempt, and His Messengers that brought them (contrary to the Law of Armes and Nations) imprisoned; That those miserable distractions, which have rent and torne this flourishing Kingdome, are so farre from being closed, that they are rather made wider; That the Sword of War, so long devouring, is not yet sheathed, except in one anothers bowels; That this Kingdome is still made the Scene of Murthers, Rapines, Oppression, and Plunderings, and whereon all the horrid acts of rage, and injustice are every day acted; and the Nation put almost out of hope, ever to enjoy her former Peace and Plentie, is *our* fault, and *ours* wholly: Had not the *root* of this Rebellion been animated by this Citie, and encouraged

encouraged by promises of more Supplies of Men and Monies, they had long before this laid down their Armes, and come with halters about their neckes, and cast themselves at the Kings feet, submissively begging those Pardons, which they have presumptuously rejected: Time was, when the *two Houses* gave a Law to the *Citie*, now it is come to that passe, that the *Citie* prescribe to the *Reliques* of the two Houses; They must not conclude of *War* or *Peace*, without consulting the *Citie*, if they doe, they reckon without their Host.

Nay, though *Fairfax* be utterly routed in the *North*, and *Williams*, once sirnamed a *Conquerour*, be totally defeated in the *West*, yet can they neither be *perswaded*, nor *beaten* into thoughts of Peace. On the 20th of *July* last, no longer ago, many Thousands (as the printed paper tells you) preferred a Petition to the House of Commons, presented by M. *Norbury*, of the *Cursitors* Office, and *Iohn Hst* an Atturney of *Guild-hall*, both pernicious men, which as it evidently shewes their obstinate aversion from Peace, so it is the most desperate devilish slander, that ever yet durst look the world in the face; for first, they tell the House of Commons, and in them the world, *That the King without any touch of conscience, and in defiance of God, hath raised an Armie of Papists, Outlawes, and Traitors, for Robbing, Burning, Murthering, and Destroying of His Religious, Honest, and well meaning People*. And then knowing not onely their *interest in*, but their *power over* the House of Commons, they do not so much *Petition*, as *Command* them to accept of their assistance, for the raising a new Armie, and in expresse termes prescribe unto them, and limit them to a *Committee* of their own *nomination*, for the seizing and receiving of such summes, as the *willing* shall thinke fit to offer, or they shall thinke fit to extort from the *unwilling* for this service: and that you may judge of the whole bunch, by some, they name *Pennington* the pretended Lord Maior, *Stroud* one of the five Members, *Harry Martin* Plunder-master Generall, and *Denis Bond* Burgesse of *Dorchester*, and *Patriarch Whites* own disciple, a man of a double capacitie to be a Rebell, and

and finding themselves more *alone* in these undertakings than they did imagine, like desperate Traitours, they call on the whole Kingdome, as one man, according to the intent of the late Covenant, to joyne with them in this Rebellion. And having thus taken a course to raise new Forces, on *Saturday* the 29th of *July*, at a *Common Hall*, they Voted Sir *William Waller*, *Generall* of their new intended Armie, whom to indeare the more, they interest him in the Government of the Citie, hoping that being as mad as his Ladie, he will hold up the Rebellion, as long as he can, and then be one of the last to run away; I mean not from *Battaile*, for in that he hath shewed himselfe as forward as the foremost, but from *Iustice*, and the due reward of his disloyaltie. By all which it is most evident, that this *Languishing Rebellion* had before this day gasp'd its last and given up the ghost, had not this *rebellious Citie* by its *wealth* and *multitudes* fomented it, and given it life.

If therefore *Posteritie* shall aske, who broke down the bounds to those streames of blood, that have stained this earth, if they aske, who make Libertie captive, Truth criminall, Rapine just, Tyrannie and Oppression lawfull, who blanched Rebellion with the specious pretence of Defence of Lawes and Liberties: War with the desire of an established Peace, Sacriledge and prophanation, with the shew of Zeale and Reformation. Lastly, if they aske who would have pulled the Crown from the *Kings* head, taken the Government off the hindges, dissolved *Monarchie*, inslaved the *Lawes*, and ruined their *Countrey*, say, 'Twas the *Proud, Unthankfull, Schismaticall, Rebellious, Bloodie Citie of London*; so that what they wanted of devouring this Kingdom by *cheating* and *couzening*, they mean to finish by the Sword.

That therefore these dangerous *Defluctions*, and continuall (not small *Distillations*) but *Floods* of Men, Money, Ammunition, and Armes, descending from the *Head Citie*, and *Metropolis* of this Kingdome, may not for ever dissolve the nerves, and

luxate

laxate the Sinewes of this admirable compofed Government; it will highly concerne this Nation to look about them, to undeceive themfelves, and to confult their own *Peace* and *fafetie*, by joyning with their Gracious Soveraigne, in *chaſtizing* thefe rebellious infolencies, and reducing this *ſtubburne Citie* of *London* either to *obedience* or *afhes*.

FINIS.